ANIMALS *in* DANGER

odorou

Heinemann
LIBRARY

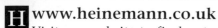
www.heinemann.co.uk
Visit our website to find out more information about **Heinemann Library** books.

To order:
☎ Phone 44 (0) 1865 888066
🖹 Send a fax to 44 (0) 1865 314091
💻 Visit the Heinemann Bookshop at www.heinemann.co.uk to browse our catalogue and order online.

First published in Great Britain by Heinemann Library, Halley Court, Jordan Hill, Oxford OX2 8EJ, a division of Reed Educational and Professional Publishing Ltd. Heinemann is a registered trademark of Reed Educational & Professional Publishing Limited.

OXFORD MELBOURNE AUCKLAND JOHANNESBURG BLANTYRE
GABORONE IBADAN PORTSMOUTH NH (USA) CHICAGO

Designed by Ron Kamen
Illustrations by Dewi Morris/Robert Sydenham
Originated by Ambassador Litho Ltd.
Printed by South China Printing in Hong Kong / China

ISBN 0431 00129 4 (hardback)   ISBN 0431 00148 0 (paperback)
04 03 02 01   04 03 02 01
10 9 8 7 6 5 4 3 2   10 9 8 7 6 5 4 3 2 1

British Library Cataloguing in Publication Data
Theodorou, Rod
    Bengal tiger - (Animals in danger)
    1.Tigers - India - Bengal - Juvenile literature
    2.Endangered species - Juvenile literature
    I.Title
    599.7'56'095414

Acknowledgements
The Publishers would like to thank the following for permission to reproduce photographs:
FLPA: Fritz Polking pg.4, Eichhorn Zingel pg.4, Jurgen & Christine Sohns pg.5, Gerard Lacz pg.6, pg.15, M Newman pg.7, Terry Whittaker pg.16, E & D Hosking pg.21, John Holmes pg.25; *NHPA*: Martin Harvey pg.26; *Oxford Scientific Films*: pg.8, Daniel J Cox pg.4, Miriam Austermanpg.9, Belinda Wright pg.11, pg.17, pg.19, pg.22, pg.24, Mahipal Singh pg.12, Mike Birkhead pg.13, Alfred B Thomas pg.14, Zig Leszczynski pg.18, Tim David pg.20; *Still Pictures*: Roland Seitre pg.23, Valmik Thapar pg.27.

Cover photograph reproduced with permission of Bruce Coleman.

Our thanks to Henning Dräger of WWF-UK for his comments in the preparation of this book.

Every effort has been made to contact copyright holders of any material reproduced in this book. Any omissions will be rectified in subsequent printings if notice is given to the Publisher.

Contents

Any words appearing in the text in bold, **like this**, are explained in the Glossary.

Animals in danger

black rhino

Florida manatee

giant panda

All over the world, more than 10,000 animal **species** are in danger. Some are in danger because their home is being **destroyed**. Many are in danger from people hunting them.

4

This book is about Royal Bengal tigers and why they are in danger. Unless people look after them, Bengal tigers will become **extinct**. We will only be able to find out about them from books.

What is a tiger?

Tigers are large **mammals**. They are the largest of the cat family. There is only one **species** of tiger, but there are five sub-species, or types.

There are the Siberian tiger, the South China tiger, the Indochinese tiger, the Royal Bengal (Indian) tiger and the Sumatran tiger. Three other types have become **extinct** in the last 70 years.

What do Bengal tigers look like?

Bengal tigers have a stripy **coat**. It is hard to see them in the shadows of the forest. This helps them to hide from their **prey** and from hunters.

Most Bengal tigers have orange, brown, black and white stripes. Some tigers have very light coloured fur. These are called white tigers.

Where do Bengal tigers live?

Bengal tigers live across the **continent** of Asia. They live in hot countries where there are long grasses and thick forests full of animals to hunt.

Bengal tigers do not like too much heat. They spend their day resting in their **dens** or under trees. They come out at night when it is cool and they can surprise their **prey**.

What do Bengal tigers eat?

Bengal tigers will eat most things but they like large **mammals** best, like deer and wild pigs. Bengal tigers also eat small mammals, birds, frogs and fish.

Bengal tigers hunt mostly at dawn or dusk when their stripes help to hide them in the shadows of tall grasses. One big meal like a deer will fill a tiger for a few days.

13

Bengal tigers like to live and hunt alone. But the **males** and **females** meet up in the spring to **mate**. The male leaves after they have mated and does not help look after the babies.

14

About three months after mating, the female will give birth to three or four babies, called cubs. She will look after them in a **den** made from plants, or in a cave or rocky area.

Looking after the cubs

When Bengal tiger cubs are born they are blind and helpless like kittens. They drink their mother's milk for three to five months. She starts to teach them how to find food.

The cubs do not hunt alone until they are 18 months old. The mother needs to protect them from adult **male** tigers, who sometimes kill cubs.

Unusual Bengal tiger facts

Unlike most cats, Bengal tigers like water and are strong swimmers. Sometimes they hunt for fish and frogs in the water. Sometimes they rest in the water to keep cool.

The stripes on a tiger's coat are like human fingerprints. No two tigers ever have exactly the same pattern of stripes.

How many Bengal tigers are there?

One hundred years ago there were about 60,000 Bengal tigers living in the wild. Now there may be as few as 4500 left.

Nowadays, the biggest number of Bengal tigers live in India. Others live in special **protected** areas called **reserves**. In China there may only be about 30 Bengal tigers left.

21

Why is the Bengal tiger in danger?

Bengal tigers are in danger from humans who hunt and kill them. The hunters make money by selling the tiger skins and bones.

Tiger bones are used in some kinds of medicines believed to cure aches and pains. Tiger skins and teeth are made into expensive clothes and jewellery and decorations like rugs.

Why is the Bengal tiger in danger?

The Bengal tigers' **habitat** is also being **destroyed**. Tigers need to live in thick forests, but the forests are being cut down to make room for farming.

Sometimes the forests are cut down to make room for factories or to build houses for people. Without the forests there are no animals for the tigers to hunt for food.

How is the Bengal tiger being helped?

Bengal tigers are now **protected** by **law**. **Conservation** groups like the World Wide Fund for Nature (WWF) work to stop people hunting and selling tiger skin and bones.

Conservation groups also work with governments to make new tiger **reserves**. Tigers can live in these reserves, safe from hunters. If they are not hunted tiger numbers might begin to rise again.

Bengal tiger factfile

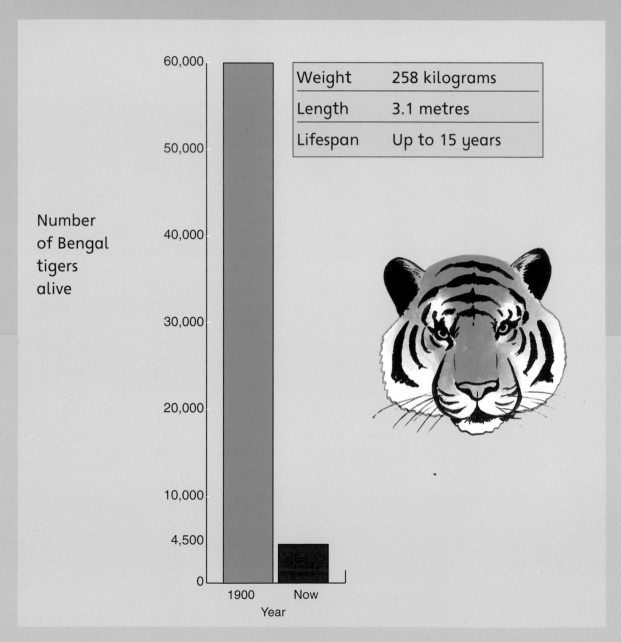

Number of Bengal tigers alive

Weight	258 kilograms
Length	3.1 metres
Lifespan	Up to 15 years

60,000

50,000

40,000

30,000

20,000

10,000

4,500

0

1900   Now

Year

World danger table

	Number that may have been alive 100 years ago	Number that may be alive today
Giant panda	65,000	650
Blue whale	335,000	4500
Black rhino	1,000,000	2000
Mountain gorilla	85,000	500
Florida manatee	75,000	1400

There are thousands of other animals in the world that are in danger of becoming **extinct**. This table shows some of these animals.

Can you find out more about them?

further reading, addresses and websites

Books

I didn't know that only some big cats roar, Claire LLewellyn, Aladdin Books Limited, 1999.

People or Wildlife? Earth Watch series, Terry Jennings, A & C Black, 1992

The Atlas of Endangered Species, John A. Burton, David and Charles, 1991

The Tiger, Junior Survival Library, Caroline Brett, Boxtree, 1992

Vanishing Species, Green Issues series, Miles Barton, Franklin Watts, 1997

Organizations

Friends of the Earth: UK - 26-28 Underwood Street, London N1 7JQ
☎ (020) 7490 1555
Australia - 312 Smith Street, Collingwood, Vic 3065 ☎ 03 9419 8700

Greenpeace: UK - Canonbury Villas, London, N1 2PN ☎ (020) 7865 8100
Australia - Level 4, 39 Liverpool Street, Sydney, NSW 2000 ☎ 02 9261 4666

WWF: UK - Panda House, Weyside Park, Catteshall Lane, Godalming, Surrey GU7 1XR ☎ (01483) 426 444
Australia - Level 5, 725 George Street, Sydney, NSW 2000 ☎ 02 9281 5515

Useful Websites

www.bbc.co.uk/nature/
The BBC's animals site. Go to Really Wild for information on all sorts of animals, including fun activities, the latest news, and links to programmes

www.bergen.org The American Smithsonian Institution site includes amazing facts about the tiger.

www.bornfree.org.uk
Virginia McKenna's site has the latest information on campaigns to save gorillas, tigers, and other animals.

www.sandiegozoo.org
The world-famous American San Diego Zoo's site. Go to the Pick an Animal section for games and factsheets.

www.tigerfdn.com
The Tiger Foundation's site includes information on how you can help save the tiger.

www.wwf.org
The World Wildlife Fund For Nature (WWF) is the world's largest independent conservation organization. The WWF conserves wildlife and the natural environment for present and future generations.

Glossary

coat	the hair covering an animal's body
conservation	looking after things, especially if they are in danger
continent	a large area of land, unbroken by sea, that can include many countries
den	place where wild animals live or hide
destroyed	spoilt, broken or torn apart so it can't be used
extinct	a species that has completely died out and can never live again
female	the opposite of a male, such as a girl or woman
habitats	the home or place where something lives
law	a rule or something you have to do
male	the opposite of a female, such as a boy or man
mammals	warm-blooded animals, like humans, that feed their young on their mother's milk
mate	when a male animal and a female animal come together to make young
prey	animals that are hunted and killed by other animals
protected	looked after, sometimes by law
reserves	a park or large area protected by guards that look after the animals
species	a group of living things that are very similar

Index